WE'RE STRANGERS HERE

WE'RE STRANGERS HERE

by Eric Chappell

JOSEF WEINBERGER PLAYS

LONDON

WE'RE STRANGERS HERE
First published in 2004
by Josef Weinberger Ltd
12-14 Mortimer Street, London, W1T 3JJ

ISBN 0 85676 276 8

WE'RE STRANGERS HERE was first presented by the Lightweight Theatre Company on August 21st, 2003 at the Theatre in the Park, Strode Park, Herne, with the following cast:

DAVID/ROBERT   Ian Soundy

AMY/LINDA   Sue Bailey

Directed by Norman Holness

Designed by Tim Liggins

Lighting designed by Mike Bennell

The play is based on an original one act television play for ATV starring Geraldine McEwan and Ian Hendry and which was later adapted into the telvision sitcom entitled *Duty Free*, starring Keith Barron, Gwen Taylor, Neil Stacey and Joanna Van Gysegham.

WE'RE STRANGERS HERE can be performed with either four actors or two.

ACT ONE

LINDA *and* ROBERT HAMMOND'S *hotel room. Spain. A summer evening in the mid-1960s. The room is decorated in Moorish style. There is a balcony upstage left which is partly out of vision. The balcony overlooks the hotel terrace and the sea. A door upstage centre leads to bathroom. A second door, stage right, leads to corridor.*

Upstage is a double bed and door to clothes closet. Downstage are two easy chairs and a coffee table with bowl of fruit. There is a dressing table stage left. There is a phone by the bed. ROBERT HAMMOND *is putting a golf ball across the carpet into a wine glass. He is about fifty, tall, well groomed, pencil thin moustache, glasses. His blazer has been placed carefully on the back of a chair.* ROBERT *addresses the ball.*

ROBERT   (*low voice*) This for the Championship. A four footer that Hammond has been sinking all through the tournament. He has one hand on the claret jug, can he make it two? Trevino and Nicklaus look devastated as well they may, they've both had their chances. Now it's the turn of the Englishman. The coolness of this talented amateur who only took up the game two years ago has shaken them. Here it is, a little right to left, to bring the Championship back to England after so many years . . .

        (ROBERT *putts.*)

        Bugger!

        (LINDA *emerges from bathroom. She is younger than* ROBERT, *about forty, attractive and elegant. She is still in her evening clothes. She regards him curiously.*)

LINDA   Were you talking to yourself?

ROBERT   No.

LINDA	I heard a voice.
ROBERT	It's these walls. Paper thin. I don't know why we came back here.
LINDA	You liked it last time.
ROBERT	It's gone downhill.
LINDA	The walls haven't got any thinner.
ROBERT	We had a better room last time.
LINDA	I thought you were going to have a drink with Toby instead of fidgeting around here.
ROBERT	I wasn't fidgeting. I was putting.
LINDA	As far as I'm concerned that's fidgeting. (*Pause.*) Well, aren't you going?
	(ROBERT *looks at his watch.*)
ROBERT	It is rather late.
LINDA	That hasn't bothered you before. You were drinking until three last night.
ROBERT	I know but the truth is I think Toby's a bit peeved . . .
LINDA	Why should he be a bit peeved?
ROBERT	They rather expected to dine with us tonight.
LINDA	Did they?
ROBERT	Instead we dined with that couple.
LINDA	Do you mean David and Amy?
ROBERT	Yes.
LINDA	You can remember their names?

ROBERT	Of course I can.
LINDA	But you make a point of not doing.
ROBERT	I'd have preferred to have dined with the Reynolds.
LINDA	Why?
ROBERT	They're more our type.
LINDA	Then God help us.
ROBERT	Why do you say that?
LINDA	I came here to get away from people like the Reynolds.
ROBERT	What's wrong with them?
LINDA	Everything. She just echoes what he says. And he only talks about that night over Bremen, or Hamburg, or Dresden – flying on a wing and prayer with nothing on the gauges but the maker's name. Not very tactful when you're sitting next to a party of Germans.
ROBERT	I don't suppose they understand.
LINDA	Of course they do, Robert. They've taken the trouble to learn our language. And Toby knows that. He means them to understand.
ROBERT	Oh, I don't think so.
LINDA	Don't you? When that elderly German from Hamburg asked him if he'd visited his city – Toby said, "Yes, every Monday and Friday night in a Lancaster bomber."
ROBERT	(*chuckles*) I thought that was rather good.

LINDA   I thought it was rather insensitive. He's still
           fighting the war, Robert – and he's not the
           only one.

ROBERT   Well, if you don't find his conversation
           interesting, talk about something else.

LINDA   I've tried that but like all bores he doesn't
           listen. When I talk he waits, as if one of those
           bloody Lancaster bombers is passing
           overhead, and then continues to talk, as if he
           hasn't heard me, about something that
           happened twenty years ago.

ROBERT   Well, you have to bear with him a little, Linda.
           He had a bad war. An eye, part of an arm, and
           I'm not too sure about the leg . . . Never wears
           shorts. And when his leg struck the table the
           other night there was a certain hollow ring. He
           gave his all, Linda. And when they finally
           brought him down over Bremen the blighters
           tried to hang him from a lamp post. You don't
           forget things like that.

LINDA   Well, I'm sorry he had a bad war. I'm sorry
           there are parts of him scattered all over
           Germany and that they tried to hang what was
           left. But since he's made the world safe for
           democracy can't we enjoy it a little instead of
           being reminded of it all the time?

ROBERT   Not all the time, Linda.

LINDA   All the time. He took his eye out and put it in
           my wine glass at lunch. I couldn't eat a thing.

ROBERT   That was just his sense of humour.

LINDA   Well, it may have seemed funny in Stalag Luft 7
           but not now. I'm never sure what part he'll
           remove next. I was going mad until David and
           Amy arrived.

           (ROBERT *studies her.*)

ROBERT   Is that why you've changed your mind?

LINDA   Changed my mind?

ROBERT   You didn't like it here. You wanted to go to Madrid.

LINDA   Yes.

ROBERT   Now you don't.

LINDA   No.

ROBERT   Quite a change . . .

LINDA   Aren't you going down to see Toby? I thought you were planning something for tomorrow. Going under the wire, or digging a tunnel, or something.

ROBERT   (*smiles*) Actually, we were planning a dawn raid.

LINDA   A dawn raid?

ROBERT   An early morning swoop on the sun beds. The Germans are putting their towels out far too early – well before breakfast. Well, after breakfast tomorrow they'll find them floating in the pool.

LINDA   Well, that should make for a pleasant week. And I thought when we were up in the mountains with them drinking sangria together and singing *Lili Marlene*, all was forgiven.

ROBERT   Don't you believe it. You'll have noticed they sang much louder than we did.

LINDA   So what?

ROBERT   I think they were trying to raise Hitler.

LINDA   That's no reason to throw their towels in the
                pool.

ROBERT   It was Toby's idea. He's brought in a few like-
                minded spirits. I asked David if he was
                interested but of course he wasn't.

LINDA   What do you mean – of course he wasn't?

ROBERT   National Service.

LINDA   What has that to do with it?

ROBERT   Never heard a shot fired in anger.

LINDA   I think David was right not to get involved. It'll
                only cause unpleasantness.

ROBERT   You might be right. (*Pause.*) If you feel like
                that perhaps we should move on . . .

LINDA   (*curiously*) Why are you so keen to move on?

ROBERT   The thunderbox hasn't worked properly since
                we got here.

LINDA   Is that all? It hasn't worried you until now.
                Besides, the man across the corridor was very
                sweet. He said if you were desperate you
                could use his.

ROBERT   (*appalled*) The Frenchman?

LINDA   Yes.

ROBERT   I didn't come all this way to use a Frenchman's
                lavatory.

LINDA   Then stop complaining – go down to the bar
                and have a nice chinwag with Toby.

ROBERT   (*hesitates*) What are you going to do?

LINDA   I'm going to assume the lotus position.

(*She takes up the lotus position.*)

During which I hope to achieve inner tranquillity. A state of mind that may prevent me having a screaming fit. If that doesn't work I shall take a stroll along the beach.

ROBERT   Again?

LINDA   What do you mean, again?

ROBERT   You did that last night.

LINDA   Yes?

ROBERT   And you went in the sea.

LINDA   Yes. How did you know?

ROBERT   I felt your bathing costume this morning, it was wet, and your beach towel.

LINDA   You felt them to see if they were wet. Are you checking up on me?

ROBERT   No, of course not. They were draped over the balcony – and they don't like towels draped over the balcony. So I moved them.

LINDA   They? Who are they?

ROBERT   (*sighs*) The hotel management. They feel it spoils the look of the hotel – and I agree with them. There's a notice up about it. I've mentioned it to you before and you agreed they were right. But whenever I go to golf I look back and there's your towel draped over the balcony.

LINDA   I keep forgetting.

ROBERT   It's not like you, Linda. You're normally the soul of correctness.

LINDA	It's the heat. I think I'm going native.
ROBERT	It doesn't seem to have affected anyone else. It's a rule observed by the Germans, the Dutch, the French, even the Italians. But not you.
LINDA	I'll try and remember in future. (*Pause.*) Well, aren't you going to plan the dawn raid?
ROBERT	Right.

(*He starts to cross to the door. Stops.*)

If you're going to the beach tonight . . .

LINDA	Yes?
ROBERT	I wouldn't.
LINDA	What does that mean? If you're going to the beach tonight – I wouldn't?
ROBERT	There are some pretty unsavoury characters about, Linda.
LINDA	Unsavoury? Surely not at this hotel.
ROBERT	Not here – but that bar on the beach. Carlo's or Pepe's or something . . .
LINDA	Pedro's?
ROBERT	You know it?
LINDA	No. I've heard it's a dump.
ROBERT	It is. They serve tortillas and sangria and serve rotgut wine – attracts the wrong element.
LINDA	I'll keep away.
ROBERT	Then how did you come by these? Book matches. Pedro's.

(He shows her the book matches.)

LINDA   A man at the hotel gave them to me. He said it was a dump.

ROBERT   Did he?

           (She studies him.)

LINDA   Do you know, Robert – that sounded almost like a trap . . .

ROBERT   What?

LINDA   Carlo's or Pepe's – have you been there? – and then the dramatic revelation about the book matches.

ROBERT   It wasn't dramatic.

LINDA   But it was a trap?

ROBERT   *(uneasily)* No. I just wondered how you came by them, that's all.

           (She gives him a level stare.)

LINDA   And now I've told you.

ROBERT   Yes. *(Pause.)* I still wouldn't go on the beach. A bus load of Italians came in this evening. Looked like a mafia outing.

LINDA   I saw them. I like the Italians. One of them called me the lovely signorina and kissed my hand.

ROBERT   That doesn't mean anything. They can't see a woman's hand without darting on it like a bird of prey. My aunt was once goosed by an Italian in front of the Vatican – and that was during a papal blessing. Better off with your own kind, Linda.

LINDA   Like Toby Reynolds?

ROBERT   We were lucky to have met them.

LINDA   That wasn't luck, Robert. You only have to see
                 a blazer, a badge, and a regimental tie and
                 you're halfway across the room. Then it's pull
                 up a sandbag, sit down and we're off. It's
                 boring.

ROBERT   They may be boring, Linda but at least they
                 served King and country.

LINDA   When are you going to get it into your head,
                 Robert, that we all served King and country.
                 The Germans bombed the shit out of our road
                 on a nightly basis.

ROBERT   (*shocked*) Linda – really.

LINDA   Just as Toby Reynolds bombed the shit out of
                 them. But we were civilians – we didn't get the
                 blazers and the badges. And we didn't go into
                 suspended animation in 1945. We got on with
                 our lives. And that's what those Germans are
                 doing.

ROBERT   They're getting on with their lives all right.
                 But they haven't forgotten – simply gone to
                 ground. That elderly German you mentioned.
                 How do we know? He could have even been –
                 certainly bore a marked resemblance to him –
                 older, of course – but who knows . . .

LINDA   What are you talking about?

ROBERT   After he'd gone Toby and I exchanged a glance
                 and our lips framed the same words . . .

LINDA   What words?

ROBERT   Martin Borman.

LINDA	(*stares*) Martin Borman. You don't think Martin Borman's holidaying here?
ROBERT	He'd have to holiday somewhere. Why not here?
LINDA	For one very good reason. He's dead.
ROBERT	Never found the body.
LINDA	Robert, either the heat's getting to you, or it's Toby Reynolds. Perhaps you should see less of him.
ROBERT	You mean see more of David.
LINDA	He's a refreshing change.
ROBERT	He's certainly not a man I'd expect to find here.
LINDA	Really?
ROBERT	Hardly five star. Not his sort of place. Out of his depth.
LINDA	Is he?
ROBERT	For one thing he doesn't appear to have any visible means of support.
LINDA	Oh. Are you referring to a lack of braces or something else?
ROBERT	I had the impression he was out of a job. Then there are the shoes . . .
LINDA	Shoes?
ROBERT	You can learn a great deal from a man's shoes.
LINDA	And what have you learnt?
ROBERT	Always wears the same pair.

LINDA	Perhaps he's fond of them.
ROBERT	Hardly. There's a hole in one of them. I noticed it the other day when he threw one leg over the other. He noticed my glance, looked embarrassed and straightened up. I had the distinct impression the hole had been filled with cardboard. Then there's the question of his cuffs . . .
LINDA	What about his cuffs?
ROBERT	Frayed. I must say he certainly looks the worse for wear – even his sunglasses are cracked. Now what's a man with a hole in his shoe – frayed cuffs – and cracked sunglasses doing in a hotel like this?
LINDA	Holidaying?
ROBERT	You know what I mean.
LINDA	You don't think he's one of those unsavoury types who goes to Pedro's, eats tortillas and drinks rotgut wine.
ROBERT	He could be. He certainly doesn't eat at the hotel if he can help it. They never take lunch.
LINDA	Perhaps they're not hungry.
ROBERT	(smiles) Oh, they eat but they don't take lunch.
LINDA	You're being very mysterious, Robert.
ROBERT	They smuggle food out of the dining room at breakfast.
LINDA	Are you sure?
ROBERT	I've been watching him. He has numerous pockets in his shirt. First it's the rolls – then

the hard boiled eggs – pats of butter –
sometimes meats – even fish. You must have
noticed how corpulent he looks when he leaves
the room.

LINDA   I haven't been watching him quite as closely as
you have, Robert.

ROBERT   He knows I'm on to him. I kept him talking in
the sun when he came out from breakfast. I
could sense his discomfort. The butter in his
pocket began to melt and run down his shirt –
and there was a distinct whiff of kippers.

LINDA   Wasn't that unkind?

ROBERT   It's against the rules, Linda. There's a notice
up about it. If he couldn't afford this place he
shouldn't have come here.

LINDA   How did you know he was out of a job?

ROBERT   Something Amy said.

LINDA   It would be.

ROBERT   Don't you think it was rather reckless coming
here – under the circumstances.

LINDA   Perhaps he felt like being reckless. He's a
romantic.

ROBERT   Is he?

LINDA   Amy's the practical one. She always brings
him down to earth – whenever he tries to soar.

ROBERT   Does he soar?

LINDA   He would do – if she let him. They're
opposites. He's a romantic – she's grim reality.

ROBERT   I suppose someone has to face the facts.

LINDA
She enjoys facing facts. She's another one who can't let go of the past, Robert. With her it's the mean streets of her childhood. She can't forget them. Well, I came from those same mean streets and I couldn't forget them quickly enough.

ROBERT
I must say she does talk politics a great deal – and she insulted Franco tonight. I wouldn't be in her shoes if he got hold of her.

LINDA
I wouldn't be in Franco's shoes.

ROBERT
She doesn't appear to like you very much, does she?

LINDA
Why do you say that?

ROBERT
I don't know – the way she looks at you every time you say something – sort of hostile.

LINDA
It's not personal, Robert. We're capitalists. My jewellery alone is enough to set her teeth on edge.

ROBERT
I thought it may be because you're always playing tennis with David.

LINDA
We like playing tennis. You don't and Amy's no good at it.

ROBERT
I don't know how you can do it in this heat.

LINDA
We stop for breathers.

ROBERT
Even so. Remember the Dutchman? He played in the heat. Went up for a high smash – came down horizontal. Had to fly the body home. Not that they could afford to fly David home – probably end up buried in a wall. That's what they do out here. Not a pleasant thought.

LINDA
Oh, I don't know – you seem to be enjoying it.

(*There's a silence between them. Noises off.*)

ROBERT   What was that?

(*He crosses to the balcony and looks down at the terrace.*)

Good Lord! You won't believe this. Someone's thrown a shoe from one of the balconies – and they're still eating on the terrace. Could have killed someone. It's landed in that chap's paella! Looks as if someone's had a row . . . Must be the heat.

(*He returns to* LINDA.)

They're not getting along, are they?

LINDA   Who?

ROBERT   David and Amy.

LINDA   Aren't they?

ROBERT   I think that's why they came here. Why they've been reckless.

LINDA   Why is that?

ROBERT   I think they came here to save their marriage.

LINDA   That's very shrewd of you, Robert – you could be right.

ROBERT   But it's not working.

LINDA   It isn't?

ROBERT   They're always having words. You must have noticed.

LINDA   Not particularly.

ROBERT   I did try to talk to David about it.

LINDA	(*stares*) You did?
ROBERT	You see, I think I've spotted the problem.
LINDA	Problem . . . ?
ROBERT	Yes. It's a mistake most couples make when they're not used to the climate. They come here for a second honeymoon and overdo things on the first day.
LINDA	(*appalled*) Is that what you told him?
ROBERT	Yes.
LINDA	What did he say?
ROBERT	He looked surprised. I don't think it occurred to him. I said, twenty minutes the first day – forty minutes the second day – an hour the third. Then, if he feels up to it, as much as he likes, with the usual precautions.
LINDA	What are you talking about, Robert?
ROBERT	The sun. They get burnt – can't bear to touch each other – bang goes the second honeymoon.
LINDA	Oh. I see. (*Pause.*) Did he think it was good advice?
ROBERT	I think he took it on board. (*Frowns.*) Although I think it goes deeper than that . . .
LINDA	Deeper than the sunburn?
ROBERT	Oh yes – much deeper. I think he feels trapped. Coming here's unsettled him. Glamorous women – hardly anything on – whiff of the bougainvillaea. He's become bored with his marriage. Pity we're not at home. I could have let him have a book on it.

LINDA   (*stares*) You have a book on it?

ROBERT   Yes.

LINDA   (*pause*) Have you read it?

ROBERT   Of course I've read it.

LINDA   And you think he's bored with Amy?

ROBERT   The signs are obvious. His attention to you –
            and the others . . .

LINDA   Others?

ROBERT   Other women.

LINDA   I hadn't noticed.

ROBERT   You aren't there. I met them in the army. Spot
            them a mile off.

LINDA   Who did you meet in the army?

ROBERT   Womanisers.

LINDA   David?

ROBERT   Never stops. We were on the terrace by the
            pool – reading our newspapers. I'd managed to
            buy a two day old *Telegraph* and he'd
            scrounged a *Daily Mirror*. This Danish girl
            walked by. Tall, blonde, bikini. Down came the
            paper – then the remark.

LINDA   What remark?

ROBERT   Fancy a little Danish pastry, Robert?

LINDA   (*pause*) Perhaps he was hungry.

ROBERT   No. It was obvious what was on his mind. He
            was alluding to the Danish girl.

LINDA   Do you know she was Danish?

ROBERT   Well, no but she looked it.

LINDA   So you were looking at her too?

ROBERT   Well, yes.

LINDA   Then perhaps she was on your mind.

ROBERT   He didn't stop there – once he was in the
                mood. A moment later – big, strapping German
                woman. Down came the newspaper – then the
                remark, "How's that for apple strudel?"

LINDA   Was it lunchtime?

ROBERT   Yes.

LINDA   He was hungry. He probably said, "how about
                a little apple strudel?" His mind was on food.
                You misunderstood.

ROBERT   I didn't misunderstand about the French girl.
                The one with the painted toenails – goes
                topless when the attendants aren't looking.
                She passed – another nudge in the ribs. "What
                about a little Ooh la la, Robert?" And you
                can't eat Ooh la la. He was inviting me to join
                him in a little male voyeurism.

LINDA   Well, it's perfectly harmless.

ROBERT   Not in my book.

LINDA   Is that the book you have at home?

ROBERT   Yes. I told him I was a married man. I had
                certain principles.

LINDA   That must have stopped him in his tracks.

ROBERT   Hardly. It was then he said the most incredible
            thing.

LINDA   What incredible thing?

ROBERT   He said he used to have principles until he
            woke up one morning in 1965 and found they'd
            gone – completely vanished.

LINDA   He was teasing you, Robert.

ROBERT   He could have been. Toby has a theory about
            it.

LINDA   You discussed it with Toby?

ROBERT   Yes.

LINDA   You shouldn't have done.

ROBERT   I don't see why not. Toby's a shrewd old bird.
            He thought it might have been a diversion.

LINDA   What?

ROBERT   A feint – a move to put me off the scent.

LINDA   What scent?

ROBERT   While I think he's chasing after the Danish
            pastry and the apple strudel, etcetera, he's
            really after someone else . . . Someone closer . . .

LINDA   Do you mean me?

ROBERT   It hasn't occurred to you?

LINDA   No. It's ridiculous.

ROBERT   I don't see why. You're not without appeal.

LINDA   Thank you.

ROBERT   And he's obviously the type. He has a roving
              eye. Probably done it before – probably doing
              it now – all over the place – probably never
              stops. He's probably unfaithful even when
              he's being unfaithful – if you see what I mean.

LINDA   What makes you think he interested in me,
              Robert?

ROBERT   He plays tennis with you all the time.

LINDA   He admires my backhand.

ROBERT   Does he?

LINDA   He raves about it. He's never known a woman
              with a backhand like mine. He said with a
              backhand like mine I should have had children.

ROBERT   You see – he was getting round to it again.
              And it's not just the tennis. He has these
              wandering hands . . .

LINDA   Well, I suppose they go with the roving eye.

ROBERT   I noticed them at dinner tonight.

LINDA   You mean they kept sneaking across the table?

ROBERT   He was all over you.

LINDA   All over me? You mean I was totally
              enveloped? I don't remember.

ROBERT   I mean every time he made a point he gave your
              wrist a squeeze.

LINDA   I didn't notice.

ROBERT   Amy did. That's when she produced the
              photographs of the children.

LINDA   That didn't mean anything. She's always
              producing photographs of the children – she's

one of these earth mothers. I can just see her
at home in a long cotton dress – children
hanging from her like wombats – and not a po
in the house emptied.

ROBERT   I think she brought them out for a reason – to
remind him of his responsibilities. Shortly after
that she insulted Franco. That was probably a
diversion.

LINDA   No, she's that sort of woman, Robert.
Everything's a debate. When we had our
picture taken with the monkey – was it fair to
the monkey? They keep it in chains and file its
teeth. Well, if they filed its teeth how did it
mange to bite your ear, Robert? I notice she
never asked if the monkey was being fair to
you. Then it was the bullfight. Was it fair to
the bull? Of course it wasn't fair to the bull – it
would have sooner been copulating with cows
in a meadow. But it was a bullfight for God's
sake, and you can't have a bullfight without a
bull.

ROBERT   All the same – I think it all springs from
jealousy – of you and David.

LINDA   Do you think I encourage him?

ROBERT   Of course not. (*Scornfully*.) A man like that?

LINDA   What do you mean – a man like that?

ROBERT   He couldn't keep you in nail polish.

LINDA   Is that what it comes down to – money?

ROBERT   I know one thing about money, Linda. It
becomes more important the less you have.
And when you haven't got any it becomes very
important. And he hasn't got any.

LINDA   (*pause*) I thought you were going to see
Toby?

ROBERT   What are you going to do?

LINDA   Remove my make-up.

                  (*She enters bathroom.*)

ROBERT   (*hesitates*) Right. See you later then . . .

                  (*He regards the bathroom door, a prey to
                  conflicting emotions, jealousy, suspicion,
                  uncertainty. He crosses to the outer door. He
                  opens it and closes it with a slam. He crosses
                  and steps inside the closet closing the door
                  behind him.*)

                  (LINDA *returns from the bathroom. She is
                  carrying a towel which she hangs over the
                  balcony. She crosses to check her appearance
                  in the mirror. She stiffens and looks towards
                  the closet. She crosses and listens at the door.
                  She returns to the balcony, removes the towel
                  and places it on a chair.*)

                  (*She crosses to the closet and opens the door.*
                  ROBERT *backs out of the closet carrying
                  several shirts. He places them on the bed
                  without a word. Crosses to the closet and
                  returns with several pieces of luggage.* LINDA
                  watches him in silence.)

LINDA   (*finally*) What are you doing?

ROBERT   Packing.

LINDA   I thought you were going to the bar?

ROBERT   I was. Then I thought I'd make a start on the
                  packing.

LINDA   We're not leaving until next week.

ROBERT   I thought you wanted to leave earlier.

LINDA   I told you – I've changed my mind.

ROBERT   Still, I can make a start. No need to leave it all
               to the last minute.

               (*He surveys the case.*)

               If I remember correctly – it's coats, suits,
               jackets, large case. Shirts, dresses, middle
               case. Underwear, socks, ties, small case.
               Beachwear, shoes, large grip. Valuables,
               documents, passports, shoulder bag. Large
               items on the bottom, small items on the top.

               (LINDA *regards the bed.*)

LINDA   There's only one small prob, Robert. Where do
               I sleep?

ROBERT   Oh. Am I in your way?

LINDA   Yes. Would you put them all back in the closet
               – all except the middle case.

ROBERT   I suppose it is rather late . . .

               (*He begins to put the cases back.*)

               Why do you want the middle case?

LINDA   I might want to pack a few things.

ROBERT   Right. The sooner the better. I for one won't
               be sorry to leave. This place has certainly
               changed – too touristy. That's the trouble
               with these package tours – they bring in the
               wrong sort of people. It won't be long before
               there's brown ale cooling in the bidets – kiss-
               me-quick hats – and the usual loutish
               behaviour.

LINDA   Then I think we should make the most of it
               while it's still unspoilt, don't you?

ROBERT   We can't stay here forever.

LINDA   I could.

ROBERT   Dog's missing us.

              (LINDA *looks at him in astonishment*.)

LINDA   The dog? How do you know?

ROBERT   Spoke to him on the phone.

LINDA   You talked to a dog – on the telephone?

ROBERT   Yes. Well, Mrs Davey put him on. Apparently
              he's been moping and she thought my voice
              would reassure him.

LINDA   And did it?

ROBERT   Yes. He started to wag his tail.

LINDA   Did you ask him what the weather was like?

ROBERT   How could I do that?

LINDA   He may have said – ruff!

ROBERT   Apparently they're enjoying a heatwave. So
              we may as well be there as here.

LINDA   You mean go back to the same old thing?

              (*He regards her moodily.*)

ROBERT   Does that include me? Am I the same old
              thing?

LINDA   Yes. You're not only the same old thing there
              – you're the same old thing here. When you're
              not playing golf you're looking for battlefields
              – always some scene of bloody conflict –
              where the Nationalists massacred the
              Republicans – where the Republicans raped

and pillaged the Nationalists. There are other
things . . .

(*She crosses to the balcony.*)

Someone's playing a guitar down there on the
beach – they're baking clams over a driftwood
fire – there's the sea and the stars. And you're
making long distance calls to a dog!

ROBERT   You mean I don't appreciate all this?

LINDA   Correct.

ROBERT   And David does?

LINDA   Yes.

ROBERT   And do you know why? It's free.

LINDA   Free?

ROBERT   The beach, the stars, the sea. All free. He
              doesn't have to pay a penny for it.

LINDA   That's true – that may even be part of their
              beauty – but what has that to do with David?

ROBERT   He's hardly bought a drink since we met him.
              He won't even buy a newspaper – gets them
              from the waste bins and if he can't do that he
              reads mine – over my shoulder – and when my
              back's turned he does the crossword. He never
              pays for a thing.

LINDA   Well, if he did, wouldn't you be disappointed?

ROBERT   Disappointed? Why?

LINDA   Because that wouldn't confirm your prejudices
              – and you like your prejudices to be confirmed,
              don't you? Besides, you wouldn't have
              anything to tell Toby.

| ROBERT | He's a sponger, Linda. I've been waiting for him to touch me for days. |

ROBERT   He's a sponger, Linda. I've been waiting for him to touch me for days.

LINDA   (*quietly*) I know the feeling . . .

(*She looks out over the balcony.*)

ROBERT   (*sharply*) What was that?

LINDA   I know the feeling of waiting to be touched.

(ROBERT *looks uncomfortable.*)

ROBERT   Well, it's too damned hot, isn't it?

LINDA   Surely not for you, Robert. Twenty minutes the first day – forty the second – then an hour with the usual precautions. And you do have a book on it . . .

ROBERT   Back's still a bit sore.

(*He studies her.*)

What's the matter? You feeling . . . you know . . . ?

LINDA   What?

ROBERT   A little . . . ?

LINDA   Yes?

ROBERT   Fruity?

LINDA   Fruity? Fruity! My God! You can't even say the words. There's a guitar playing on the beach – they're baking clams over a driftwood fire – there's the scent of sweet jasmine and bougainvillaea on the night air. And you ask if I'm feeling fruity! Is that how your friend Toby would express it? "Early night tonight, Robert – the mem sahib's feeling a bit fruity."

ROBERT   Well, I just thought . . . I meant, if you felt like that. I don't mind.

LINDA   Don't mind?

ROBERT   I don't mind not going to the bar . . . if you'd like to . . . you know . . .

LINDA   Why? It's not my birthday, is it?

ROBERT   That's not fair, Linda.

LINDA   Actually, I wasn't talking about that. I was talking about a little human warmth and understanding. I want to walk barefoot on the beach – have a drink at one of those little cafes – look at the stars. All you want to do is stick a golf ball into a sodding wine glass.

ROBERT   All right! I'll walk along the beach with you.

LINDA   It's too late.

ROBERT   Will David be walking along the beach and looking at the stars.

LINDA   He could be.

ROBERT   Then he has these finer feelings I suppose?

LINDA   Yes. He says he can sit and look at the sea for hours.

ROBERT   Well, he has the time, hasn't he? To look at the sea and the stars. He's out of work. Plenty of time for finer feelings when you have nothing to do.

LINDA   That's not the reason – he's just more sensitive.

ROBERT   Oh, he's sensitive. I saw him at the bullfight. He was white with fright – cowering in his seat

– almost fainted – all at the sight of a little blood.

LINDA   Poor David. He didn't want to see it but he felt he had to.

ROBERT   Completely ruined the afternoon – thought he was going to be sick.

LINDA   Is that why you're so eager to leave – because of David?

ROBERT   Isn't that why you're so eager to stay?

LINDA   No.

ROBERT   (*pause*) It's not my reason either . . . The truth is I've not been sleeping very well.

LINDA   Oh?

ROBERT   I've been having those dreams. I had another one last night . . .

LINDA   I don't want to hear it, Robert. I don't like your dreams – they're not very nice.

ROBERT   This one was different.

LINDA   I'm sure it wasn't. You'd be in some public place – in your pyjamas looking for a loo.

ROBERT   I wasn't in my pyjamas.

LINDA   But you were looking for a loo and you couldn't find one, or it was occupied, or there was no door on it, or there were three people trying to get in it at the same time. It's an insecurity dream. You're dreadfully insecure, Robert.

ROBERT   I wasn't looking for a loo! That wasn't what the dream was about.

LINDA   Are you sure?

ROBERT   Of course I'm sure. I was getting an ice-cream cornet from that kiosk by the pool.

LINDA   Are you sure you weren't in your pyjamas?

ROBERT   Yes. Although I did appear to have mislaid my trousers.

LINDA   That's the same thing. Insecurity.

ROBERT   As I was getting the cornet along comes David and he gets one, too.

LINDA   Was he in pyjamas?

ROBERT   No.

LINDA   Or without his trousers?

ROBERT   No. He was fully clothed.

LINDA   You see.

ROBERT   What do you mean – you see?

LINDA   He's not insecure.

ROBERT   Linda – it wasn't his dream. It was mine. How do you know what he's like in his dreams? He could be totally naked.

LINDA   Only if he was insecure.

ROBERT   As I was saying. We both bought cornets – and we ran back to you with them.

LINDA   Me?

ROBERT   Yes. And we offered you our cornets . . .

LINDA   Was I in pyjamas?

ROBERT   No! Will you stop talking about pyjamas?

LINDA   I'm sorry but does this dream have any point,
              Robert?

ROBERT   I'm coming to it. We offered you our cornets
              and you accepted David's.

LINDA   I accepted David's cornet?

ROBERT   Yes.

LINDA   Were you upset?

ROBERT   At first but then I looked down and saw that
              my cornet had melted.

LINDA   Oh dear. I can see how disturbing that must
              have been.

ROBERT   It was.

LINDA   Standing there without your trousers then
              looking down and finding your cornet had
              melted . . .

ROBERT   I knew you'd laugh. It's not funny.

LINDA   You think the dream has some deeper meaning?

ROBERT   Don't you?

LINDA   Have I done something to make you dream like
              that?

ROBERT   It's not what you've done. It's the way it
              looks.

LINDA   How does it look?

ROBERT   People are talking.

LINDA   Talking? To you?

ROBERT   No, not to me. They've said things to Toby.

LINDA   Oh, we're back to Toby again.

ROBERT   He's been talking to some of the recent arrivals
            – they think you're married.

LINDA   I am married.

ROBERT   To David.

LINDA   What?

ROBERT   They've seen you playing tennis – and walking
            – and swimming and dancing . . . they think
            you're a married couple. How do you think
            that makes me feel? You being mistaken for
            another man's wife?

LINDA   Toby should mind his own business.

ROBERT   I wish he had but he hasn't. Then he showed
            me this photograph. He's just had them
            developed.

            (*He takes photograph from his jacket pocket.*)

            He took it at Pedro's – they were having a
            disco. Toby was after a little local colour. He
            certainly found it. He was shocked.

LINDA   Was he?

ROBERT   So was I.

            (*He shows her the picture.*)

            See the couple dancing in the corner? Almost
            hidden from sight but not quite. You can see
            it's David – there's not so much of you –
            you're sort of enveloped – so it's hard to tell.
            But it certainly isn't Amy . . .

LINDA   That's how people dance at discos.

ROBERT   Well that's how they dance at Pedro's . . .

LINDA   So that's Pedro's.

ROBERT   Yes.

LINDA   I didn't realise that was Pedro's. I certainly
            didn't see Toby there. Where was he when he
            took this – crouching behind a bush?

ROBERT   He was as surprised as I was.

LINDA   He wasn't. He's a dirty old man, Robert.
            Didn't you know? I've felt his good hand on
            my knee more than once. Do you know what
            this picture is – a prurient snigger. Probably
            something to do with his experiences in Stalag
            Luft 7. With my uncle it was food – never
            travelled anywhere without six loaves of bread
            after repatriation. With Toby it's something
            else.

ROBERT   You said you didn't know Pedro's.

LINDA   (*hesitates*) I knew you wouldn't approve.

ROBERT   I don't.

LINDA   There you are then. Does it matter? We were
            dancing close – so what? We're not going to
            see these people again.

ROBERT   That's it exactly. It's because they're not
            going to meet again that they behave like this.
            That and this place – the sun – the wine – the
            scented breezes. Take the English woman next
            door. Looked perfectly respectable when she
            arrived. Now every night it's, "Stop it,
            Miguel."

LINDA   You can hear her?

ROBERT   Through the wall.

LINDA	Who's Miguel?
ROBERT	The wine waiter.
LINDA	Oh. He's rather nice.
ROBERT	How can you say that? How can you say he's nice? When she's saying, "Stop it, Miguel."
LINDA	Does he?
ROBERT	What?
LINDA	Stop it?
ROBERT	Of course he doesn't stop it. She wouldn't keep saying, "Stop it, Miguel" if he stopped it.
LINDA	(*pause*) What do you think he's doing?
ROBERT	What do you think?
LINDA	Does she say anything else?
ROBERT	Sometimes, "Don't, Miguel" but usually it's, "Stop it, Miguel". Then there's silence.
LINDA	A silence?
ROBERT	Yes.
LINDA	Do you think that's when he's doing whatever she's been telling him to stop doing?
ROBERT	Could be. The point is what is he going to think of us?
LINDA	(*stares*) What does it have to do with us?
ROBERT	She's English – we're English. It rubs off. He'll have a pretty low opinion of us now.
LINDA	Oh, I don't know.

ROBERT   I thought I detected a certain smugness from
              him at dinner.

LINDA   I thought that was because they'd beaten us at
              football.

ROBERT   No, I think he'd triumphed in a very different
              field of sport.

LINDA   And you think she's let the side down?

ROBERT   Don't you?

LINDA   Perhaps you think I'm letting the side down?

ROBERT   (*hesitates*) Not intentionally – but in a way.
              You've changed since you got here – you're
              not the same.

LINDA   That's it, Robert. You've put your finger on it.
              I'm not the same – but you are. You haven't
              changed. And when I see you with strangers I
              see you through their eyes. At home it's
              different. Everyone knows you. They accept
              you. I accepted you. But here I see you
              through the eyes of other people.

ROBERT   And what do you see?

LINDA   I see an overblown, pompous English cabbage.

ROBERT   A cabbage!

LINDA   A cabbage amongst olives, oranges, grapes
              and other exotic fruits. An English cabbage –
              that's how they see you.

ROBERT   Is that how David sees me?

LINDA   I don't know how David sees you. It's how I
              see you. And you can't be a cabbage out here,
              Robert – you'll wilt.

ROBERT	You're in a very strange mood tonight.
LINDA	You're like Amy, Robert. You've brought all your luggage with you. And I'm not talking about three cases, two grips and a shoulder bag. She's brought her prejudices with her just as you've brought yours. With her it's Franco and the fascists – with you it's how we stuffed it up them at El Alamein.
ROBERT	My God! Suddenly I'm in the wrong. Why is it that whenever I think I'm in the right I suddenly find that I'm in the wrong?
LINDA	Because you are.
ROBERT	And I suppose Amy's in the wrong, too.
LINDA	She doesn't understand him.
ROBERT	And you do?
LINDA	Yes. How can she understand him when she doesn't understand herself? She thinks she's their conscience – that she's out to reform the world but she's not. All she wants to do is keep him firmly in his place and weigh him down with all the cares of life. That's the only way she can be sure of him. She's impossible.

(*He regards her in silence for a moment.*)

ROBERT	You realise what you're saying? You're making a very good case for avoiding them in future.
LINDA	Only Amy – unfortunately they're a pair – you can't have one without the other.
ROBERT	At least not at dinner . . .
LINDA	What?
ROBERT	Perhaps if you saw less of David she wouldn't dislike you as much.

LINDA   She doesn't dislike me because of David. It's
             because she's sensed I've escaped from those
             mean streets. She thinks I've become grand.
             Well, in 1947 I fetched coal for my mother in an
             old pram. I walked through the town with it.
             And I could do it again. I've never been too
             proud. I know what it's like to be poor. It
             wasn't nice.

ROBERT   Then it's lucky you met me, isn't it?

LINDA   Oh. So we're back to the dosh again?

ROBERT   No.

LINDA   You married me – you didn't buy me.

ROBERT   I know.

LINDA   Why don't you go down to the bar and join the
             rest of the cabbages?

ROBERT   What are you going to do?

LINDA   I shall look at the sea . . .

             (*She crosses to the balcony and out of sight.*)

ROBERT   Right. I'll go down then . . .

             (*He crosses to pick up his blazer then stops.
             He glances towards the balcony and then
             crosses to the outer door, opens it and slams it
             shut as before. This time he tiptoes into the
             bathroom and closes the door gently behind
             him. A moment later* LINDA *slowly emerges
             from the balcony. She looks cautiously
             around the room. Crosses and checks the
             closet. Satisfied, she picks up the towel and
             places it on the balcony. She checks her
             appearance in the mirror. She suddenly
             becomes aware of* ROBERT'S *blazer still on the
             back of the chair. Becomes thoughtful. She*

crosses and listens at the bathroom door and then enters. She returns looking thoughtful. There is a gleam of realisation. She returns to the bathroom. Sound of shower being switched on . . . muffled cry, off. LINDA *returns flicking spots of water from her hand. She folds her arms and watches the bathroom door.*)

(ROBERT *enters from the bathroom looking drenched but trying to maintain his dignity. Silence.*)

LINDA   (*quietly*) Did you want something, Robert?

ROBERT   I was looking for a dry towel.

LINDA   There's one over there.

                 (*He crosses and takes towel from the balcony and begins to dry himself. Stops and stares at towel.*)

ROBERT   Strange – the towel's on the balcony again.

LINDA   You think that's strange? Do you normally take a shower with your clothes on?

ROBERT   I wasn't taking a shower. You switched it on.

LINDA   I didn't know you were lurking in the shower, did I? Still, it makes a change from the clothes closet. Why are you spying on me, Robert?

ROBERT   Because this towel was on the balcony.

LINDA   What?

ROBERT   It's a signal, isn't it?

LINDA   A signal?

ROBERT   That the coast's clear. Then it's either meet me
                here – or meet me there. I don't know where – I
                haven't worked that out yet.

LINDA   You're talking nonsense.

ROBERT   Should we see?

                (*He replaces the towel on the balcony. They
                regard it for a moment.* LINDA *crosses and
                removes the towel.*)

ROBERT   Ah, so it was meet me here.

LINDA   They don't like us to hang out towels from the
                balcony – you said so yourself.

                (ROBERT *grows in confidence.*)

ROBERT   That hasn't worried you before. But then I
                wasn't here before, was I? I was safely out of
                the way. You've been seeing him whenever
                this towel's been hung from the balcony. And
                the towel's been on the balcony a great deal.
                Don't bother to deny it. It's true, isn't it?

LINDA   (*pause*) Yes.

ROBERT   Caught you nicely, haven't I?

LINDA   Have you?

ROBERT   You're a clever woman, Linda – but I'm not
                exactly stupid.

LINDA   Not exactly, no.

ROBERT   Well, I'm going to do you a favour. I'm going
                to stop a clever woman making a fool of
                herself. You won't see him anymore. We'll
                check out tomorrow.

LINDA   We won't, Robert. Because I'm leaving
                tonight.

ROBERT	What?
	(LINDA *begins throwing her things into the suitcase.*)
LINDA	That's why I asked you to leave the case. I wasn't sure if I was going to pack it – that rather depended on you.
ROBERT	Depended on me?
LINDA	On how much of a stuffed shirt you were going to be.
ROBERT	Stuffed shirt!
LINDA	That's what I said – stuffed shirt. And you exceeded my wildest expectations. I'm leaving.
ROBERT	You can't. Where would you go?
LINDA	Madrid.
ROBERT	Madrid! (*Laughs.*) How will you get there – on foot? You won't have the car.
LINDA	I don't need it. I reserved a hire car. It's out there waiting.
ROBERT	What!
LINDA	I've split the traveller's cheques. I have my passport. There's nothing to stop me.
ROBERT	You've planned this.
LINDA	I thought it might come to it.
ROBERT	You mean if I found out. And is David going to Madrid?

LINDA   I haven't asked him but he'd be welcome. In
                 any event I'm going. I should have left years
                 ago.

ROBERT   You did, twice. And you came back.

LINDA   Not this time. I've dug for affection, Robert –
                 until the spade broke. I don't feel like trying
                 again.

ROBERT   There you are, you see. I'm in the wrong
                 again. You're leaving – walking out of our
                 marriage – and I'm in the wrong.

LINDA   What marriage? This isn't a marriage. We're
                 just fellow travellers, Robert. I'll send for the
                 rest of my things.

                 (*She shuts case. Crosses to the fruit bowl.*)

                 Oh, and if you're feeling fruity tonight . . .

                 (*She hands him a lemon.*)

                 Suck a lemon.

                 (*Blackout. End of Act One.*)

ACT TWO

AMY *and* DAVID PEARCE'S *hotel room. Same place. Same time. The room is identical to the Hammond's except the drapes may be a different shade with different ornaments and pictures.*

AMY *is moving in and out of the bathroom preparing for bed. She is in her thirties. She is attractive but an air of watchful cynicism has hardened her looks.*

DAVID *is standing on the balcony looking out to sea. He is older than* AMY *but acts younger. He has removed his shoes and loosened his tie and is puffing on a cigar. He is clearly not in the mood to go to bed.* AMY *gives him an irritated glance.*

AMY	Aren't you coming to bed?
DAVID	Not yet.
AMY	What are you doing?
DAVID	Looking at the sea.
AMY	Haven't you seen enough of it?
DAVID	I never get tired of looking at the sea.
AMY	It's only water, David.
DAVID	How can you say that? That's the Mediterranean out there.
AMY	You're not flicking your ash on the people below, are you?
DAVID	No. (*Pause.*) I've always had this feeling for the sea. Do you know, the first time I saw it, it had barbed wire in it? It was just after the war. That was the North sea. It was green and cold and had barbed wire in it, in the waves. I've half expected to find barbed wire in it ever since . . .

(AMY *emerges from bathroom in pyjamas. She crosses and stares at* DAVID.)

AMY   That's weird.

DAVID   What is?

AMY   Barbed wire in waves. That's really Freudian.

DAVID   Is it?

AMY   I'd really worry about thoughts like that.

      (*She crosses to the dressing table.*)

DAVID   (*dryly*) Would you?

      (*He turns his attention back to the sea.*)

      The next time I saw it, it was off the South Coast. That was warmer. I was only a boy but I still remember swimming by this couple and hearing the woman say, "Kiss me in the water, Philip." Just like that. "Kiss me in the water..."

      (DAVID *becomes lost in reverie.*)

AMY   (*pause*) Well, did he?

DAVID   What?

AMY   Kiss her in the water?

DAVID   Oh yes. They kissed passionately and disappeared beneath the waves.

      (*She regards him thoughtfully.*)

AMY   What made you think of that?

DAVID   I don't know. Just came to me.

      (*He looks back at the sea.*)

It's very still out there, Amy. No white horses tonight.

AMY   No white horses. Do you mean waves? You normally say waves.

(DAVID *frowns and abandons the balcony.*)

DAVID   What's the matter with you?

AMY   Nothing.

DAVID   Didn't you enjoy this evening?

AMY   No.

DAVID   I can't understand that. I thought we had a terrific evening.

AMY   (*darkly*) Didn't you sense an atmosphere?

DAVID   No. (*Pause.*) Was there an atmosphere?

AMY   Didn't you notice how silent Robert became?

DAVID   Well, yes . . . but I thought it was a comfortable silence.

AMY   How do you know that?

DAVID   What?

AMY   You've only known him a few days. How do you know if his silence was comfortable or uncomfortable?

DAVID   Well, you know Robert. He puts words together like someone threading beads.

AMY   Well, he didn't thread many beads tonight, did he?

DAVID   He's a good listener. He likes to listen.

AMY

How do you know? He could have been dying to speak. Words could have been choking him. (*Pause.*) I think he was silent for a reason . . .

DAVID

What reason?

AMY

Don't you know?

DAVID

No.

AMY

I didn't like the way he was looking at you.

DAVID

Looking at me. For God's sake, Amy. Do you have to do this?

AMY

Do what?

DAVID

Analyse everything. Couldn't you just enjoy the moment?

AMY

You mean like Linda?

DAVID

Yes. She enjoyed this evening.

AMY

She was pickled.

DAVID

She was not.

AMY

Pickled as a walnut.

DAVID

You mean because we had a few laughs and she found me amusing?

AMY

She didn't find you amusing. That grin was fixed. You couldn't have removed it with a drill.

(DAVID *throws his hands in the air.*)

DAVID

Amy, where have you been this evening? You couldn't have been with me.

AMY

Why did you keep touching her all the time?

(DAVID *stares at her in surprise.*)

DAVID   I didn't.

AMY   It was very noticeable. You're becoming quite
          a toucher these days, David. Your eyesight's
          not failing, is it?

DAVID   (*coldly*) No.

AMY   Are you sure? You were running your hands
          over her like Blind Pew. Still, she didn't seem
          to mind. You don't think she's a
          nymphomaniac, do you?

          (DAVID *almost chokes on his cigar and stubs it
          out violently.*)

DAVID   Of course not.

AMY   How do you know? Just because you haven't
          met one before doesn't mean they don't exist.
          They're rare – like the white rhino or the snow
          leopard . . . probably as dangerous, too.

          (AMY *sits back on the bed and takes out some
          holiday cards.* DAVID *watches her for a
          moment and then begins to look around the
          room.*)

DAVID   Where are my shoes?

AMY   Why do you want your shoes?

DAVID   (*hesitates*) I thought I'd take a last look at the
          sea . . .

AMY   Not again! Have you any idea what time it is?

DAVID   I'm not tired. I haven't felt tired since I got
          here. It's this place – it's so different. Listen
          – someone's playing a guitar down on the
          beach. There's the scent of sweet honeysuckle
          and bougainvillaea on the night air and the

sound of cicadas. You don't get that in
England, Amy.

AMY   I saw our milkman this morning.

(DAVID *turns in surprise.*)

DAVID   What, here?

AMY   Yes. I saw him bobbing up and down in the sea
– just his head.

DAVID   Are you sure?

AMY   Well, he didn't have his milk float with him but
I recognised him. We waved to each other.

DAVID   (*doubtfully*) Our milkman couldn't afford this
place.

AMY   Neither can we, David. If it wasn't for your
redundancy we wouldn't be here.

DAVID   (*sharply*) Don't say that.

AMY   It's true.

DAVID   We don't want people to think we find this
place expensive.

AMY   Don't we?

DAVID   And I don't want people to know I'm
unemployed. You haven't told anyone?

(AMY *looks uncomfortable.*)

AMY   No. (*Pause.*) It's nothing to be ashamed of.
There are plenty of people unemployed.

DAVID   That doesn't mean I have to be one of them. I
was on a low salary at that company for twenty
years because it was a safe job. Safe! I never
went abroad. Everyone from the office went

abroad. Oh, yes. They went to Italy, Germany, France. I'd find them around the coffee machine smoking Gauloise and talking about Montmarte. And I couldn't even afford a day trip to Bologne.

(AMY *looks regretful for a moment.*)

AMY

I'm sorry, David. I didn't mean to bring it all back.

DAVID

(*bitterly*) Didn't you? I'll tell you something now. When we flew over the bay into Malaga and I saw the blue Mediterranean and those little white house . . . I almost cried.

(*He turns away and looks ferociously for his shoes.*)

AMY

(*quietly*) I didn't know you felt like that, David.

DAVID

How could you? You're not interested. You know you're trouble – you're too provincial.

AMY

Am I? Why do you say that?

DAVID

When we went up into the hills today – you refused to enjoy yourself, didn't you?

AMY

I've been on a donkey before, David.

DAVID

Burro, Amy. They're called burros. It wasn't Weymouth sands – they were the Sierras – stretching endlessly before us – distant rocks seem to hang in the air forever. As I rode along I felt the slow heart beat of old Spain. And then at the hacienda when we drank sangria from a barrel and ate paella – and sang Lillie Marlene with the Germans – there seemed to be no boundaries. I thought that was a very healing moment . . .

AMY   Did you? That was their marching song. If
           there'd been a brass band they'd have been
           ready to invade Czechoslovakia.

DAVID   There you go again.

           (AMY *considers*.)

AMY   Provincial?

DAVID   Yes. And you make me feel provincial.

AMY   Are you sure it's me who makes you feel
           provincial, David?

DAVID   What do you mean?

AMY   They've been everywhere, haven't they?

DAVID   Who?

AMY   Linda and Robert.

DAVID   Yes.

           (*He crosses and looks out to sea.*)

           They went to Pompeii last year. That must
           have been something.

AMY   Yes, I heard her talking about it.

DAVID   She told me that they came across this couple
           in the ruins, locked in a passionate embrace . . .

AMY   Those Italians – you'd have thought they
           could have waited.

DAVID   No – they were dead.

AMY   (*stares*) Dead?

DAVID	They were engulfed in volcanic lava two thousand years ago. It's believed they were making love when the volcano erupted.
AMY	Well, that's certainly being caught with your pants down.
DAVID	Linda said it was rather beautiful. She said they must have been lost in ecstasy – not caring if the world ended – and when it did, they were locked in an immortal embrace forever.
	(*He looks dreamily out to sea.* AMY *gives a long, low laugh.*)
	What's so funny?
AMY	Who says they didn't care? Did she knock on the rock and ask them? I know it's very nice but I wouldn't want to be doing it for two thousand years. That must be the longest shag in history.
DAVID	Do you have to be so crude?
AMY	I didn't introduce the subject of fossilised sex. She talks about it a lot, doesn't she?
DAVID	What?
AMY	Sex. That's when she's not assuming the lotus position. Have you seen her on the beach – all in knots – staring up her own backside? She looks like a stranded squid.
DAVID	She's trying to achieve inner tranquillity.
AMY	That's what I thought. I thought that woman is trying to achieve inner tranquillity. And the way she looks at things, have you noticed?
DAVID	Yes – she tries to look at things as if for the first time.

AMY   That's what I thought. I thought that woman is
               looking at things as if for the first time. A
               piece of coral – a sea shell – looking at it for
               the first time with the eyes of a child. Have
               you noticed the eyes of a child?

DAVID   Do you have to be quite so sarcastic?

               (*He moves away.*)

               Where are my shoes? They were here a
               moment ago.

AMY   You should look after them. You're the only
               person I know who'd try to cross Europe in one
               pair of shoes.

DAVID   That's not my fault. I thought you'd packed
               the others. And I can't afford to buy another
               pair. (*Sighs.*) One pair of shoes – and one of
               those has a hole in it. They'll think I walked
               here.

AMY   Just keep you feet firmly on the ground, David.
               I know that's difficult.

DAVID   It certainly is.

               (*He crosses to the mirror and undoes a button
               on his shirt.*)

               Look at the chest. I'm glad I worked out before
               we came. Look at the tan – see how it makes
               the teeth gleam? When I was on the beach this
               morning – leaning against a boat – I was taken
               for a fisherman.

AMY   You weren't.

DAVID   A local fisherman. They asked me about the
               tides – in Spanish. Of course I couldn't reply
               but it was quite a moment. I haven't looked so
               good in years.

(*He surveys himself.*)

They say a man renews himself every seven years.

AMY   What?

DAVID   He renews himself. Skin, hair, cell tissues, everything. Every seven years.

AMY   You're not talking about the seven year itch, are you?

DAVID   No. I'm saying I've renewed myself.

AMY   You don't look any newer to me. You just look seven years older. But then the sun can be very ageing.

(DAVID *turns away from the mirror.*)

DAVID   I've noticed something lately, Amy. You never say anything nice to me.

AMY   Yes, it worries me sometimes. I seem to have lost the art of the compliment.

(DAVID *glances towards the mirror.*)

DAVID   (*musing*) Funny thing about bodies – they don't age like faces. We seem to grow older downwards . . . I've watched people on their balconies when they're changing – looking unexpectedly glamorous in their underwear – almost like film stars . . .

AMY   Do you do much of that?

DAVID   What?

AMY   Watching people changing?

DAVID   No. It just makes me wonder how much
             glamour's hidden under coats and sweaters in
             England. I suppose it's the climate here.

AMY   Well, you've certainly found a new lease of
             life. Races in the pool, beach games, press-
             ups. I didn't even know you could do press-
             ups. Is it to impress Linda?

DAVID   I'm not trying to impress Linda.

AMY   Are you sure? I've seen wire-haired terriers
             with more self-control. In fact, when she's
             being particularly nice to you I half expect you
             to roll on your back and throw your feet in the
             air.

DAVID   Do you? Well, Linda and I are having what is
             known as a good time. That's what you're
             supposed to do on holiday. But not you. You
             can't do that. You have to be serious.

AMY   What do you mean?

DAVID   All we wanted tonight was a little frivolity but
             not you. You wanted to talk politics.

AMY   All I said was –

DAVID   I know what you said.

AMY   All I said was that it was a dictatorship.

DAVID   (concerned) Amy – they don't think of it as a
             dictatorship.

AMY   Why have you lowered your voice?

DAVID   I haven't lowered my voice.

AMY   It's a dictatorship – just like Greece.

DAVID   Good. We'll go there next year and you can
             insult them.

AMY	You're not prepared to face the truth.
DAVID	We're not here to face the truth – we're on holiday.
AMY	Why won't Picasso come back?
DAVID	I don't know.
AMY	Because Franco's a dictator.
DAVID	Will you keep your voice down.
AMY	And Pablo Casals won't play here, because there's no freedom. It's a dictatorship.

(DAVID *glances nervously towards the balcony*.)

DAVID	(*hisses*) All right! But it's a benevolent dictatorship.
AMY	If it's benevolent – why are you whispering?
DAVID	Because I don't want to upset people. You don't know who's listening.
AMY	You're right. They have spies everywhere.
DAVID	They don't have spies everywhere.
AMY	What about the man at the airport who kicked my suitcase? Sidled up and kicked my suitcase.
DAVID	(*stares*) Why should he do that?
AMY	Probably looking for a bomb.
DAVID	(*sighs*) Amy, if there'd been a bomb it would have blown his foot off. Look, it may not be our form of government but it works.

AMY   No it doesn't. Remember when we were out the
               other day and we couldn't finish our packed
               lunch? And I gave it to those children. They
               were thin.

DAVID   God – now the children are thin. Amy, they're
               made that way.

AMY   They were so thrilled – they had tears in their
               eyes. They fetched their parents – they
               wanted me to have wine in their little hut – they
               held my hands. All over some fruit and a few
               tomatoes. And they're their tomatoes really . . .

DAVID   I don't remember any of this.

AMY   No – you and Linda were too busy admiring the
               view.

DAVID   Yes – and I don't want to hear how thin the
               children were. They were probably gypsies.

AMY   Oh, that's all right then – it's fine if they have
               to live off a rubbish dump.

DAVID   You don't know that. I agree with Linda. We
               don't visit a country to criticise it. It's bad
               manners.

AMY   What have bad manners got to do with it? If a
               thing's wrong –

DAVID   Who do you think you are? Joan of Arc? We
               don't know what goes on here. We're
               strangers.

               (AMY *regards him for a moment.*)

AMY   We're strangers everywhere these days, David.

DAVID   You were certainly a stranger to me tonight. I
               could see Linda was embarrassed.

AMY	She wasn't embarrassed. She wasn't listening to what I was saying. She was too busy flirting with that little wine waiter.
DAVID	(*frowns*) I didn't see her flirting.
AMY	Oh? I thought that was why you were rude to him.
DAVID	I wasn't rude to him.
AMY	Then why did he throw you the five?
DAVID	(*stares*) Throw me the five? What are you talking about?
AMY	When they make that gesture with their fingers. (*Gestures.*) It's called throwing the five. It's an old Mediterranean custom – particularly amongst waiters.
DAVID	What does it mean?
AMY	Five sorts of bad luck.
DAVID	What?
AMY	You should have thrown it back at him.
DAVID	How could I? I didn't know about it.
AMY	Throw it back at him tomorrow – in the meantime, don't take any chances . . .
DAVID	What do you mean – don't take any chances?
AMY	Risks of any kind. Not a time to attempt any new enterprise . . .
DAVID	I'll have a word with that waiter.
AMY	You can't blame him. She's a flirt.
DAVID	She's not.

AMY	She is. If there was no-one else in the room she'd flirt with the sideboard. She's a man-eater. She was probably exercising her vaginal muscles all through dinner.
DAVID	(*angrily*) Will you shut up about her? So we were enjoying a mild flirtation. What's wrong with that?
AMY	What's wrong? You're married.
DAVID	You think I don't know? You never cease to remind me. It was perfectly harmless.
AMY	Was it? Then why did you think of the barbed wire tonight?
DAVID	What?
AMY	The barbed wire in the waves. That spells danger, David. The steel beneath the damask silk – reaching for a rose and grasping a thorn.
DAVID	My God! We're back to Freud again.
AMY	You're afraid she'll make a fool of you, aren't you, David?
DAVID	(*bitterly*) You're forgetting something. I've been made a fool of. My week's work is now being done in ten minutes by a computer. I'm washed up, Amy. Getting to know an attractive woman is about the only excitement I've got left.
AMY	Well, get to know me.
DAVID	I know you.
	(*He turns away from her.*)
AMY	Well, watch out for Robert.

DAVID	Why?
AMY	Didn't you see those big fists opening and closing tonight? He could turn ugly if he were crossed . . .
DAVID	He doesn't love her. They aren't happy.
AMY	Oh. She told you that?
DAVID	She said she dug for affection until the spade broke.
AMY	That sounds like her. You don't believe all that little girl lost stuff, do you? Listening to sea shells – walking barefoot – looking at driftwood with the eyes of a child – seeing things as if for the first time. Looking into the distance and sighing. She's as hard as nails.
DAVID	She is not.
AMY	(*pause*) Attractive. What's attractive about her?
DAVID	Nice figure.
AMY	I've had children.
DAVID	You wanted children.
AMY	Oh, and what did you want – the family allowance?
DAVID	Linda would have liked children.
AMY	Would she?
DAVID	But she said she couldn't face bringing them into this sort of world with its horrors and ugliness and the prospect of nuclear war.
AMY	You're sure it's not because she was frightened of losing her figure?

DAVID   Of course not.

AMY   Perhaps you're right. It wouldn't have been
                 much of a loss, would it?

DAVID   What do you mean?

AMY   Well, there's not much of it, is there? Too
                 much dieting – and the trouble is it always
                 goes from the face . . . And of course you can
                 be too slim... I mean, your bones can start to
                 stick out . . . then you just look thin . . . She
                 went topless on the beach the other day and no
                 one noticed.

DAVID   I didn't see her.

AMY   There you are, you see. It was a non-event.

DAVID   My God! This is all because I paid her a few
                 compliments. Can't you give it a rest?

AMY   David, you can't expect me to sit quietly by
                 while the good ship Matrimony is in danger.

DAVID   If you're talking about our marriage I'd say
                 what it lacks at the moment is trust and
                 understanding.

AMY   We have those, David. You trust me and I
                 understand you.

DAVID   And I understand you. I know what you really
                 dislike about her – it's because she's got
                 money.

AMY   Yes, because that's what you like about her.

DAVID   Now it's her money! I saw you looking at her
                 rings. I thought you were going to take out an
                 eyeglass.

AMY   I suppose it's an advantage to carry your
            wealth on your fingers – especially in a foreign
            country. So handy in times of flight . . .

DAVID   What?

AMY   She can always peel a ring off and throw it to
            the servants.

DAVID   That's typical.

AMY   What is?

DAVID   That you should think I'm attracted to her
            wealth. It couldn't be that she's attractive.
            No, it had to be something you can't compete
            with, like money.

AMY   Am I competing?

DAVID   (*uneasily*) No.

            (AMY *sits back on the sofa.*)

AMY   Come here, David.

            (*He joins her reluctantly.*)

            If I'm jealous – there's a reason. This was
            supposed to be our second honeymoon. Our
            first holiday without the children.

DAVID   I know.

AMY   I can smell the bougainvillaea too, David. I can
            hear the cicadas. Can't we share them?

DAVID   I suppose so.

AMY   (*closer*) Think of it, all those little
            grasshoppers rubbing their back legs together,
            just for us . . .

            (*She kisses him.*)

Do you remember our first night? I was so
nervous.

DAVID   (*grins*) I don't know why. We had enough
           rehearsals . . .

           (*They lean back into the cushions. DAVID'S
           smile turns into a frown. He sits up and takes
           a pair of shoes from behind the cushion.*)

           My shoes! You hid them.

AMY   I don't know how they got there.

DAVID   Yes, you do. You put them there. Just to stop
           me going for a walk.

AMY   I don't want you to go, David.

DAVID   I've gathered that. And if you'd asked me I
           wouldn't have gone. But no – you had to be
           devious. Well, now I'm going . . .

AMY   No.

           (*Whilst* DAVID *is slipping on one shoe she
           grabs the other one.*)

DAVID   Amy, give me that shoe.

AMY   No.

           (*She backs towards the balcony.*)

DAVID   (*advancing*) Give it to me. I'm warning you . . .

AMY   You're not going . . .

           (*She continues to back away.* DAVID *makes a
           sudden lunge. She throws the shoe over the
           balcony.*)

DAVID   (*appalled*) Amy! What have you done?
         They're still dining on the terrace. You could
         have killed someone.

         (*He peers cautiously over the balcony.*)

         Oh my God!

AMY   (*nervously*) What is it?

DAVID   It's fallen into someone's food. They're
         examining it.

         (*He retreats quickly.*)

         What am I going to say?

AMY   Don't say anything. They won't know whose
         it is.

DAVID   Of course they'll know. They only have to
         look for a man with one shoe!

         (AMY *peers over.*)

AMY   I'll retrieve it later. When the fuss has died
         down.

DAVID   (*anxiously*) Are they making a fuss?

AMY   A shoe descends from the sky and plummets
         into someone's food? Of course they're
         making a fuss. Now come to bed and help me
         with these cards.

DAVID   I can't concentrate. How could you do such a
         thing? I'm sweating. I could do with a swim.

AMY   The pool's closed.

DAVID   (*hesitates*) There's always the sea.

AMY   I wouldn't.

DAVID   Why not?

AMY   It's full of jelly fish.

DAVID   No it isn't.

AMY   One floated up to me this morning. It was
              hideous – swollen and wrinkled.

DAVID   It was a carrier bag.

AMY   It wasn't.

DAVID   It was a carrier bag – it had duty free written all
              over it.

AMY   Well, I wouldn't take any chances, David –
              their sting can be fatal.

DAVID   Nonsense – there's nothing more refreshing
              than a midnight swim . . .

              (*She regards him thoughtfully.*)

AMY   You went for a midnight swim last night, didn't
              you? After I'd gone to bed.

DAVID   (*hesitates*) Yes, I did as a matter of fact. It
              was so warm and inviting. It was like rich red
              wine.

AMY   You didn't drink any of it, did you?

DAVID   What do you mean?

AMY   You were gone a long time. When did you get
              back? It must have been late. I was asleep.

DAVID   Oh, about one.

AMY   It was two o'clock, David. Where did you swim
              to – Gibralter? (*Pause.*) And did Linda go for a
              swim?

DAVID	(*defiantly*) Yes – actually, it was her idea.
AMY	So the sea wasn't the only thing you found warm and inviting.
DAVID	Look, if I'd asked you, you wouldn't have come in.
AMY	I can't swim, David. I'd drown.
DAVID	You don't try.
AMY	My bathing cap fills up with water and I sink like a stone.
DAVID	You wouldn't sink like a stone – not in the sea. The salt water makes it buoyant. Like the Dead Sea – you can't sink in that.
AMY	I'd sink.
DAVID	You wouldn't. Linda told me. She's been in the Dead Sea.
AMY	Ah, that explains it.
DAVID	What?
AMY	Must have stayed in too long.
DAVID	Don't start on Linda again.
AMY	(*pause*) David, if I did drown, would you be sorry?
DAVID	Of course I'd be sorry.
AMY	Would you weep at the funeral and cry, "Too late, too late"?
DAVID	I don't know about that.
AMY	Would you keep my clothes?

DAVID   Why should I keep your clothes?

AMY   To remind you. So that you could open the
             wardrobe and inhale my fading perfume.

DAVID   I hadn't thought about it.

AMY   Would you marry again?

DAVID   (*sighs*) Amy, I haven't got over the drowning
             yet – give me a moment. (*Pause.*) There'd be
             the children to consider . . .

AMY   Yes. Would you wait six months?

DAVID   Of course.

AMY   What about a year?

             (DAVID *thinks about it.*)

             Don't answer that – I'll settle for six months.

             (AMY *turns her attention to the cards.*)

             Is there anyone you want to send a card to?

DAVID   No, I don't want people to think we're sending
             out cards just because we're abroad.

AMY   I was only thinking of family.

DAVID   Don't forget Bob Slater.

AMY   Who's Bob Slater?

DAVID   You know. Met him two years ago at
             Weymouth. Pompous – full of his own
             importance – biggest sandcastles on the beach.
             We couldn't stand him.

AMY   Then why are we sending him a card?

DAVID	Because he sent us a card from Malta last year. And mark our balcony with a cross. I want him to know we've got a sea view. And don't forget Tommy Wright.
AMY	Tommy Wright?
DAVID	We were at school together.
AMY	David, you haven't seen him in twenty years.
DAVID	Tommy and I were going to travel the world together.
AMY	Where is he now?
DAVID	Peterborough. You've got the address. I want him to know I haven't lost the old wanderlust.
AMY	Well, if you're going to send a card to Tommy – I might send one to Aubrey Broadbent . . .
DAVID	(stares) The butcher?
AMY	Yes. Mother says he often asks after me.
DAVID	Why?
AMY	Why? You know why. You know how he felt about me. They say the bottom fell out of his world when I married you. (Pause.) I just hope this won't arouse his interest again . . .
DAVID	Then why send it?
AMY	I just don't want him to think I've stagnated. I won't send it if you don't want me to.
DAVID	No, I don't mind.
AMY	You're not jealous?

DAVID   Of Aubrey Broadbent? His face is red from
         years in the deep freeze. Some people say he's
         never thawed out.

AMY   What should I say to your mother?

DAVID   Oh. Weather fantastic – food excellent – hotel
         superb. Having a wonderful time.

AMY   Are we, David?

         (*Knock on the door. They stare at each
         other.*)

DAVID   That's the management. They're going to ask
         us to leave.

AMY   Of course they won't.

DAVID   It's going to be like Cinderella. If the shoe fits
         I'm for it.

         (*He crosses to the door and opens it slightly.*)

         Ah. So that's where it got to. I was brushing
         away – off it flew. Could have gone anywhere.
         Gracias. Gracias. I'll catch you later . . .

         (*He closes the door with relief and returns
         with the shoe.*)

         They've returned it.

         (*He slips it on his foot and stands.*)

AMY   Then you're still going?

DAVID   Yes. Why not?

AMY   And will Linda be there?

DAVID   At this time of night? She'll be asleep.

AMY   Oh, I don't think Linda ever sleeps. (*Darkly.*)
               She waits . . .

               (AMY *takes* DAVID'S *hand.*)

               Come here. I want to show you something.

               (*She leads him to the wall.*)

               Do you know what that is – up there on the
               wall?

DAVID   No. What is it?

AMY   A praying mantis.

DAVID   Do you want me to swot it?

               (*He rolls up a magazine.*)

AMY   No. They call it the praying mantis because of
               its attitude of prayer. See? They say that after
               they've made love, the female bites his head
               off.

DAVID   (*pause*) No wonder he's praying.

AMY   No, I think that's the female . . . waiting . . .

               (DAVID *raises the magazine as if to strike then
               sees* AMY *watching him and lowers it again.*)

DAVID   You're not very subtle, are you?

AMY   Oh, I can be subtle.

               (*She stands in his path to the door and holds
               up a cigar packet.*)

               What's this number?

DAVID   What number?

AMY   On your cigar packet. 230.

(David *studies it thoughtfully.*)

DAVID   I don't know. Must be a reason. You don't
            put a number on a cigar packet without a
            reason . . .

AMY   That's what I thought . . .

DAVID   I know. Two-thirty.

AMY   Two-thirty?

DAVID   That's when we had to meet Linda and Robert
            – to go to the bullfight.

AMY   Oh, yes the bullfight. What a way to spend an
            afternoon.

DAVID   I must say it wasn't what I expected.

AMY   Wasn't what you expected! Well, it was
            exactly what I expected. It's the same result
            every week. Matadors Three. Bulls Nil. It's
            barbaric. And it continues because people like
            you and me go to see it.

DAVID   Yes, you made your views pretty clear at the
            time – to everyone.

AMY   Oh, and what were your views?

DAVID   Actually, I was bored.

AMY   Bored! Do you always go that colour when
            you're bored?

DAVID   What colour?

AMY   Ashen.

DAVID   I wasn't. I was bored because I thought
            there'd be more danger.

AMY   Danger!

DAVID   I don't think the matador was standing very
             close to the bull.

AMY   He was closer than you were. If you'd been
             any further back in your seat you'd have been
             behind the stands. We should never have
             gone. Wait a minute, I thought the bull-fight
             was at four-thirty?

DAVID   We had to allow time to get there.

AMY   Oh, yes. (*Innocently.*) You know before you
             explained it to me, I thought it might be a room
             number.

DAVID   A room number?

AMY   Yes, a room number.

DAVID   I can't remember any room number.

AMY   Perhaps that's why you wrote it down –
             because you couldn't remember it. Should we
             see? Two – three – nought . . .

             (AMY *picks up the bedside phone and dials.*)

             Oh, hello Robert. Is Linda there? My
             hairdryer's playing up again and . . . She's not?
             No it'll keep until morning. David? No, he's
             here. (*She smiles at* DAVID.) All tucked up. Do
             you want a word? No? See you in the morning
             then. Bye.

             (*She replaces the phone.*)

             What a surprise.

DAVID   (*uneasily*) It slipped my mind.

AMY   I thought it best to say you were in bed. He
             sounded strange.

DAVID   Strange?

AMY   Angry . . . and emotional.

DAVID   (*dryly*) Were his big hands opening and closing?

AMY   I've no idea what his hands were doing. Why did you need the number?

DAVID   I remember now. Silly really. She was alone in her room . . .

AMY   Yes?

DAVID   Robert was golfing. And I happened to be here . . . and she rang.

AMY   Why?

DAVID   She thought she'd seen something small and dark scuttle under the bed.

AMY   Really? It wasn't that little wine waiter, was it?

DAVID   I couldn't find anything.

AMY   Why didn't she ring the desk. Surely that was the correct thing to do?

DAVID   I don't know.

AMY   I mean she is a very correct sort of person.

DAVID   I wouldn't say that exactly.

AMY   Oh, I would. Does the right thing. Not one to flaunt the rules . . .

DAVID   No, I suppose not.

AMY   That's what's been puzzling me.

DAVID   Amy, where is this leading?

AMY   The hotel has a rule, David. No towels should be draped over the balconies. You can understand it – it looks so unsightly.

DAVID   Well, yes . . .

AMY   I think we all agree with that rule, don't we?

DAVID   I suppose so.

AMY   Well, would it surprise you to know that the most persistent offender is Linda?

DAVID   Is she?

AMY   Yes. Often when we're sitting by the pool I see her drape a towel over the balcony. Don't you think that's strange – for someone who's usually so correct.

DAVID   I hadn't noticed.

AMY   Oh, she doesn't leave it there for long.

DAVID   There you are then.

AMY   But here's something even stranger – something you'd hardly believe. Shortly afterwards – you disappear.

DAVID   What do you mean disappear?

AMY   You go to the bar – or a walk on the beach – or for an ice cream . . .

DAVID   So what?

AMY   You must admit it's strange.

DAVID   I'm not listening to anymore of this. You're paranoid.

AMY   Am I?

                (*He rounds on her.*)

DAVID   You've forgotten how to enjoy yourself. This
                place is wasted on you. You should have
                stayed in England. Do you know why I wanted
                to come here? To find another way of living.
                Oh, I don't mean this hotel. Have you seen
                those little courtyards with the fountains?
                They're beautiful. All we have is a shopping
                precinct and a statue of a woman with three
                holes in her? Ever seen a woman with three
                holes in her? We have a pub called the Jolly
                Beefeater that has plastic torture instruments
                on the walls and a juke box. The river's full of
                rusty prams and they lock the park up on
                Sunday. If you can't see the magic of this
                place you must have as much life and passion
                as a two day old meringue.

AMY   (*quietly*) Isn't that what's called changing the
                subject, David?

DAVID   I'm sick of the subject. I'm going.

AMY   No, you're not.

DAVID   You can't stop me.

AMY   If you go – I'll go onto the balcony and shout,
                "Death to Franco".

DAVID   (*stares*) You wouldn't.

AMY   How's that for passion?

DAVID   They'll arrest you.

AMY   Let them.

DAVID   It's your look out.

(*He turns to the door.* AMY *moves to the balcony.*)

AMY   (*shouts*) Death to Franco!

(DAVID *pulls her back into the room.*)

Death to –

(*He covers her mouth then slowly removes his hand.*)

Death – !

DAVID   (*fiercely*) All right! I'll stay.

(*He releases her. He crosses to the balcony and stares out moodily. She watches him for a moment.*)

AMY   Have a drink, David. We still have some cherry brandy left from the duty free.

(*She crosses to the sideboard and pours them both a drink. She hands him his glass. He takes it silently.*)

(*accusingly*) You've been going to her room, haven't you?

(DAVID *takes a deep breath.*)

DAVID   Yes.

AMY   Why?

DAVID   I can't explain it. These things happen. I couldn't help myself.

AMY   (*erupts*) Couldn't help yourself! Couldn't help yourself. What did she do? Bring you down with a drugged dart?

(*She begins to pace.*)

DAVID   I knew you wouldn't understand.

AMY   My God! You're not satisfied with doing it –
         you want me to understand it. You realise this
         is adultery – they stoned them for it in the
         bible.

DAVID   Yes, you'd have enjoyed that, wouldn't you?
         You should have lived in those days. You'd
         have been on the front row with the biggest
         pile of rocks you could find.

AMY   You're damned right!

         (*She picks up an ashtray and throws it at him.
         He ducks and watches with horror as it sails
         over the balcony.*)

DAVID   They'll send for the police.

AMY   That doesn't worry me. The law's on my side.
         This is a Catholic country. This is the home of
         the Inquisition, the branding iron, and the rack
         – and I wish I had them now.

         (*She throws another ashtray. DAVID ducks.*)

         I just wish she was here.

DAVID   You don't understand. She feels terrible.

AMY   She feels terrible! How do you think I feel?

DAVID   She wants to talk to you.

AMY   (*stares*) My God! I think you want us to be
         friends. You've got me on the scaffold and
         now you want me to shake hands with the
         executioner.

         (*She slumps wearily into a chair.*)

DAVID   Amy, have you finished throwing things?

AMY   (*quietly*) Yes. That was my last ashtray on the subject.

DAVID   Can we be civilised about this?

AMY   Why not? Send out for a dry martini and a long cigarette holder.

DAVID   (*pause*) I still love you, Amy.

AMY   And I love you. And I can only love once. I'm like the mute swan, David. If you love me how do you explain this?

DAVID   I love you . . . but I'm not in love with you.

AMY   Is there a difference?

DAVID   I was in love with you once . . .

AMY   You certainly were. And you covered yards of Basildon Bond telling me about it. And I've still got the letters. And you promised to keep on loving me. I've got witnesses. There were eighty people at that wedding. The vicar's still alive. They all heard you. And God. What about God?

DAVID   All right, Amy. I know what I promised.

AMY   I should have listened to the vicar. He must have known something. He said, "You're embarking on the sea of matrimony – some days the sea will be rough – some days there will be storms. But one day, with God's grace, you'll reach safe haven." And that's what it's been like – fifteen years before the mast with Captain Bligh.

DAVID   Then what are you complaining about? She's not taking anything you want.

AMY   It won't last, David. This will fade with the
               suntan. She doesn't know you.

DAVID   Neither do you.

AMY   What's there to know? Getting to know you is
               like peeling an onion. You remove one layer
               only to find another. And the more you peel
               the more you weep.

               (*He turns away.*)

               I didn't mean that, David.

DAVID   Yes, you did.

AMY   You don't love her. It's because Robert's rich
               and successful. This is your revenge on
               capitalism.

DAVID   There you go again! The money! You can't
               believe I could prefer any woman to you.

AMY   What is it then? Is she more fun in bed? What
               does she do – use glove puppets or juggle six
               oranges?

DAVID   One thing she doesn't do is make me feel
               inferior.

AMY   I don't make you feel inferior – you are inferior.

               (DAVID *looks hurt.*)

               I didn't mean that.

DAVID   Yes, you did. Linda would never have said
               that. Her face lights up when she sees me.

AMY   So does mine.

DAVID   I feel her watching me . . . You don't know how
               that makes me feel.

AMY	I watch you, David.
DAVID	When?
AMY	In the morning. In the half light. You look so young. All the years seem to fall away – and I want to put my hand out and touch you.
DAVID	Why didn't you?
AMY	Because then you'd wake and remember you're out of work and start to frown. I know every part of you, David – better than she does.
DAVID	It's too late, Amy.
AMY	You're breaking my heart, David.
DAVID	Hearts don't break that easily, Amy – certainly not yours.

(*The phone rings.* DAVID *snatches up the receiver.*)

Hello? Linda? Where are you? Now calm down. What! Yes. Well, where are you now? What are you going to do? Are you sure? All right. All right. Just wait there. I'll be down in a few minutes . . . Bye.

(*He replaces the receiver. Hesitates for a moment.*)

That was Linda – she's left him.

AMY	What!
DAVID	They had a terrible row – and she walked out. She plans to go to Madrid. She has friends there.
AMY	Good.
DAVID	(*pause*) She wants me to go with her.

AMY   (*alarmed*) But you can't. We only have a few
               days left. We're going home at the end of the
               week.

DAVID   (*slowly*) I might not be coming home . . .

AMY   Of course you're coming home. I mean, what
               do I tell the children? They still believe in
               happy endings. The prince doesn't turn into a
               frog on the last page. Besides, you're half way
               through that body building course – do you
               want to be misshapen for the rest of your life?
               And what about your mother? She'll certainly
               be reaching for the tablets when she hears
               about this.

DAVID   I don't know about that. She never liked you
               that much.

AMY   What do you mean? She adores me. I've been
               like a daughter to her.

DAVID   That's not what she says.

AMY   The devious old bat. It must run in the family.
               Well, my mother never liked you either. I'll tell
               you something I've never told you before.
               When I said we were getting married – my
               mother wept.

DAVID   And I'll tell you something I've never told you
               before – so did mine.

               (*He takes out a suitcase and begins to throw
               clothes into it.*)

AMY   I should have listened to my mother – but you
               were so persistent. You wore your knees out
               begging me to marry you.

DAVID   I didn't wear my knees out. You were crazy
               about me.

AMY

Crazy about you!

DAVID

I only had to touch you and you trembled.

AMY

Trembled!

DAVID

Yes – trembled. Trembled like a . . . like an aspen leaf.

AMY

An aspen leaf! You've never seen an aspen leaf. You don't know what an aspen leaf looks like. An aspen leaf! You always were too poetical. I remember you following me on your bike reciting, "Shall I compare thee to a summer's day", and riding straight into a dustcart. Why did I do it? I could have had my pick. I was so popular. I was the centre of attention. You were just a face in the crowd – an eccentric – the cycling poet. I should have listened to my mother and married Aubrey Broadbent.

DAVID

Aubrey Broadbent! His carcasses have more life than he has. Aubrey Broadbent!

AMY

Aubrey Broadbent has a string of butcher's shops.

DAVID

Good for Aubrey.

AMY

At least he's made a success of his life – which is more than can be said for you.

(He gives her a withering look and hurls more clothes into the case.)

Oh God! I didn't mean that.

DAVID

You meant it.

(Amy sits, defeated.)

AMY

What am I going to tell people? *(Stops.)* What am I going to tell the WI?

DAVID	What have they got to do with it?
AMY	I gave them my recipe for a happy marriage at the last meeting – I wish I'd made it Quiche Lorraine.
DAVID	Amy, I don't want you to be unhappy.
AMY	It's a bit late for that, David. You know how you felt when they made you redundant and you went to bed with a bottle of whisky? That's how I feel.
DAVID	It'll happen again, Amy – you'll find happiness.
AMY	I don't want happiness – I want you, David.
DAVID	You can't make a person stay if he doesn't want to.
AMY	David, if we waited for people to want to be with us we'd all be on our own.
DAVID	I'm going, Amy.
	(*He closes case.*)
	And you can shout, "Death to Franco" as loud as you like – I won't be here.
	(*He slips on his jacket and admires himself in the mirror for a moment.*)
AMY	Well, before you go – have another liqueur.
	(*She slowly pours the dark sticky liquid over his head and shoulders. He stares at himself in horror.*)
DAVID	Look what you've done! You've ruined my jacket. (*He throws off the jacket.*) Look at the shirt. Look at my hair. You're mad.

AMY   How's that for passion, David?

               (DAVID *enters the bathroom tearing off his
               shirt. Sound of shower.* AMY *shouts above the
               noise.*)

               I shall want adequate maintenance for me and
               the children. I'm going to squeeze you until
               the pips squeak.

               (DAVID *puts his head around the door.*)

DAVID   I thought your heart was broken. I can see it's
               going to be a bloody expensive repair.

               (*Slams bathroom door.*)

AMY   I shall want the house and the car.

DAVID   (*off*) You can have everything.

AMY   That's what they all say . . .

               (*She takes the suitcase and empties the
               contents over the balcony.*)

               You can have everything. Two weeks later
               they're back for the hi-fi.

               (*She enters the bathroom and returns with the
               rest of* DAVID'S *clothes and his bathrobe. She
               hurls these over the balcony and with a final
               flourish, the shoes. She closes the case and
               puts it back on the bed.* DAVID *emerges in*
               AMY'S *bathrobe. He stares at her
               suspiciously. She gives him an innocent smile.
               He opens the case.*)

DAVID   Where are my clothes?

AMY   Aren't they there?

DAVID   Of course they're not there.

(*He stares at her and a terrible realisation dawns. He crosses and looks over the balcony.*)

You've thrown them over the balcony!

AMY   You wanted excitement, David. I'm giving you enough to last a lifetime.

DAVID   My trousers are hanging from the bougainvillaea! That was insane.

AMY   You're right, David. That was stupid. As you say, you can't make someone stay if he doesn't want to.

(*She takes some documents from her handbag and hands them to* DAVID.)

DAVID   What's this?

AMY   Your travel documents and your freedom. You can go.

(DAVID *stares from* AMY *to the balcony and back. There is the sound of raised voices from the terrace.*)

DAVID   I can go?

(*He peers over the balcony.*)

Amy, my trousers are hanging from the bougainvillaea – my underpants are in someone's soup – there's a dog running around with one of my shoes. And you say I can go? I couldn't even cross the lobby like this.

AMY   I thought you'd go through fire and flood for that woman.

DAVID   Not dressed like this!

(*The phone rings.* DAVID *snatches it up.*)

Hello? Linda. I'm sorry, there's been a delay.
What? From the bougainvillaea? (*Pause.*)
Yes, they are my trousers. Yes – and the rest
of my clothes . . . Amy. What? Have you
thought about this? You have. I know but –
Hello? Hello . . . ?

(*He replaces the phone and pauses for a
moment.*)

She rang off. Robert was with her. They're
leaving for Madrid first thing in the morning.

(*He sits down wearily.* AMY *watches him.*)

AMY	She's not going away with you then?
DAVID	No.
AMY	That didn't last long.
DAVID	(*stares*) What?
AMY	She's very changeable, isn't she?
DAVID	She said I'd never be free of you. She said it had become all so undignified.
AMY	That's us, David. We're definitely on the undignified side.
DAVID	Us! It was you. You ruined everything.
AMY	If you feel like that, you can leave.
DAVID	I'm not leaving! You've spent all night keeping me here – you're not getting rid of me now.
AMY	(*peers over balcony*) They're getting your clothes together. (*Sighs.*) It's times like this I wish you had better labels. (*Pause.*) Well, I suppose you can always sleep on the couch.

DAVID   You think so? (*Hesitates.*) I wasn't really
               unfaithful . . .

AMY   (*stares*) What?

DAVID   Not spiritually . . .

AMY   It wasn't the spiritual bit I was worried about.

               (DAVID'S *shoulders slump.* AMY *begins to draw
               the curtains across the balcony. She pauses.*)

               Do you want a last look at the sea?

DAVID   Why? It's only water, Amy. (*Sighs.*) I
               couldn't even do this right. I was supposed to
               be on a second honeymoon. I chase after
               another woman. I make a fool of myself. I end
               up losing both of them . . . what a failure.

               (AMY *comes up behind him. She puts her hand
               out to touch him, hesitates, then turns him
               towards her.*)

AMY   You're absolutely right. You've been dreadful.
               You've neglected me – you've been with
               another woman – you threatened to leave me . . .

DAVID   (*miserably*) I know.

               (AMY *defiantly fights back the tears.*)

AMY   But the point is this – are we going to let it
               spoil the holiday?

               (DAVID *stares at her in surprise. He laughs
               gently.*)

DAVID   Oh, Amy . . .

               (*He puts his arms around her. They stand
               motionless as the lights fade.*)